JAGUAR

Julia J. Quinlan

PowerKiDS press.

New York

Published in 2014 by The Rosen Publishing Group, Inc.
29 East 21st Street, New York, NY 10010

First Edition

Editor: Jennifer Way
Book Design: Greg Tucker
Book Layout: Kate Vlachos

Photo Credits: Cover © Uli Jooss/culture-ima/Age Fotostock; pp. 4–5 Fedor Selivanov/Shutterstock.com; p. 6 fritz16/Shutterstock.com; p. 7 (top) DeepGreen/Shutterstock.com; p. 7 (bottom) iStockphoto/Thinkstock; p. 8 © Transtock/SuperStock; p. 9 Bocos Benedict/Shutterstock.com; p. 10 Miguel Medina/AFP/Getty Images; p. 11 (top) Sorbis/Shutterstock.com; p. 11 (bottom) ARZTSAMUI/Shutterstock.com; pp. 12–13 Claudio Zaccherini/Shutterstock.com; pp. 14, 23 Darrell Ingham/Getty Images Sport/Getty Images; p. 15 Bryn Lennon/Getty Images Sport/Getty Images; p. 16 From http://en.wikipedia.org/wiki/File:1949_Jaguar_XK120_Roadster.jpg, CC BY SA 3.0; p. 17 hin255/Shutterstock.com; pp. 18–19, 27 (top) Car Culture/Car Culture Collection/Getty Images; p. 20 lendy16/Shutterstock.com; p. 21 © imagebroker.net/SuperStock; p. 24 Bloomberg/Getty Images; pp. 25, 28 Stefan Ataman/Shutterstock.com; p. 26 Kosarev Alexander/Shutterstock.com; p. 27 (bottom) Max Earey/Shutterstock.com; p. 29 Maksim Toome/Shutterstock.com.

Library of Congress Cataloging-in-Publication Data

Quinlan, Julia J.
 Jaguar / by Julia J. Quinlan. — First edition.
    pages cm. — (Speed machines)
 Includes index.
 ISBN 978-1-4777-0806-4 (library binding) — ISBN 978-1-4777-1192-7 (pbk.) —
ISBN 978-1-4777-1193-4 (6-pack)
 1. Jaguar automobile—Juvenile literature. I. Title.
 TL215.J3Q56 2014
 629.222—dc23
                          2012047579

Manufactured in the United States of America

CPSIA Compliance Information: Batch #S13PK8: For Further Information contact Rosen Publishing, New York, New York at 1-800-237-9932

Contents

Meet the Jaguar

Jaguars are fast, sleek, powerful jungle cats. They are beautiful and tough. They are the perfect animals to represent the British car company Jaguar. Every car made by Jaguar has a small silver jaguar roaring on its hood. Since 1931, Jaguar has been making some of the most desirable and luxurious sports cars in the world. Jaguars are classic and **innovative** at the same time. Jaguar is known for its **design** and attention to detail.

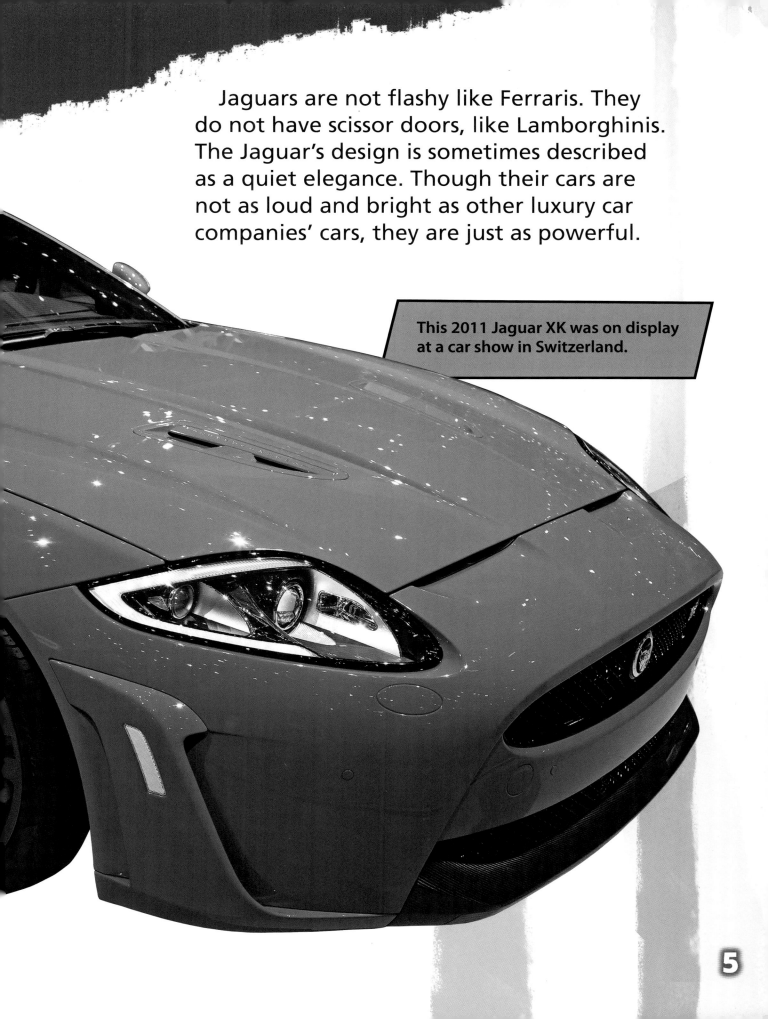

Jaguars are not flashy like Ferraris. They do not have scissor doors, like Lamborghinis. The Jaguar's design is sometimes described as a quiet elegance. Though their cars are not as loud and bright as other luxury car companies' cars, they are just as powerful.

This 2011 Jaguar XK was on display at a car show in Switzerland.

From Sidecars to Sports Cars

Jaguar may make sports cars now, but that is not how the company began. In 1922, William Lyons and his friend William Walmsley founded the Swallow **Sidecar** Company. Lyons loved motorcycles and wanted to make sidecars. Over time, the company grew and began making **chassis** for other car companies like Fiat and Austin. In 1931, the Swallow Sidecar Company joined with another company and made their first car, the SSI.

This is a 1937 Jaguar SS 100. Only about 200 of this model were made in that year.

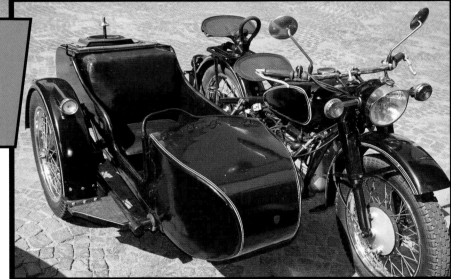

Top: This is a 1954 Jaguar XK 120 drop-head coupe, which is a type of convertible. *Right*: A motorcycle with a sidecar lets the rider carry a passenger.

The first car to be named Jaguar was made in 1935. It was called the SS Jaguar 100. Soon, they dropped the SS and changed the company to simply Jaguar.

During World War II, Jaguar went back to making sidecars for military motorcycles. After the war, in 1948, Jaguar introduced the XK120, its first **production** car. Jaguar originally planned to make only 200 of the cars. However, the XK120 was so popular that Jaguar began mass-producing them.

Aerodynamic Inspiration

An aerodynamic design like this 1958 D-Type racecar reduces the force of air pushing against the car. This allows the car to move swiftly.

Jaguar has always had more understated designs than its competitors. Their cars have always been just as powerful, though. For example, Jaguar's 2013 line of cars is both stylish and fast, with the option of choosing a powerful V8 engine. V8 means there are eight **cylinders** arranged in a V shape. The more cylinders a car has the more power the engine has.

During World War II, Jaguar helped Great Britain's war effort by making sidecars and aircraft. The company's experience making airplanes later influenced the **aerodynamic** design of its cars. In 1954, Jaguar came out with the D-Type. The D-Type was heavily influenced by airplane design. It was made with a **monocoque chassis** with a special "tub" where the driver and passenger sat. This was an innovative design at the time.

This is an example of a V8 engine. There are four cylinders on either side of the engine, and they are arranged in a *V* shape.

Evolution of a Classic

Jaguar sports cars have **evolved** over the years. Earlier Jaguars had a silver jaguar statue leaping off the hood of each car. Modern Jaguars have the face of a snarling jaguar on a small plate on their grilles. The 1948 XK120 with its two seats, long front nose, and exaggerated headlights is quite different from modern models. The 2013 XK looks edgy in comparison to older models. Jaguar always uses the most advanced **technology** and most powerful engines, and provides the best handling.

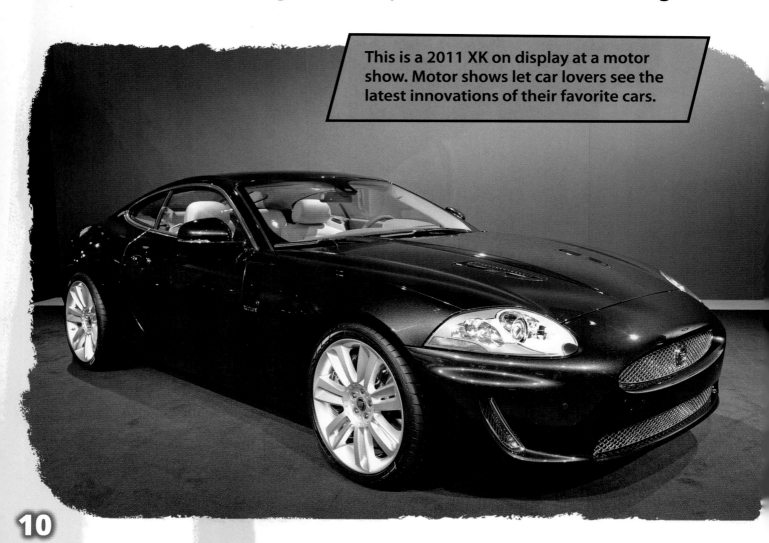

This is a 2011 XK on display at a motor show. Motor shows let car lovers see the latest innovations of their favorite cars.

Top: This is the older-style "leaping" Jaguar hood ornament. *Right*: Here is an example of the newer "roaring" Jaguar logo.

They change their cars' exteriors, or outward designs, to reflect these cutting-edge inner qualities.

Jaguar offers its customers many options when they buy a car. Customers can choose an engine, different colors, and a convertible or hard top. These choices let customers make the Jaguar that is exactly right for them.

Like most luxury sports car companies, Jaguar has made many racecars. Sports car companies make racecars to demonstrate the performance of the cars they engineer. Racecars are faster and more powerful than sports cars. They usually have differently shaped bodies and are lower to the ground so they can go faster. They are made for driving on racetracks rather than on roads.

In 1950, Jaguar entered a race called the 24 Hours of Le Mans for the first time with its XK120 model. The car was very fast but was unable to finish the race because of mechanical problems. The next year, Jaguar entered with its XK120C and won the race! The XK120C drove 2,244 miles (3,611 km) and had an average speed of 93 miles per hour (149 km/h). In 2011, Jaguar made a new car, called the RSR XKR GT2, to compete in 24 Hours of Le Mans. That model had a top speed of 180 miles per hour (290 km/h).

This 1952 XK120 is similar to the model that won the 1951 24 Hours of Le Mans.

Racing Legacy

Over the years, Jaguar has been a part of many different racing competitions. The company is most famous for its success in the 24 Hours of Le Mans races. Jaguar has won the competition seven times. They won in 1951, 1953, 1955, 1956, 1957, 1988, and 1990. The 24 Hours of Le Mans is the oldest active **endurance** car race. The race is 24 hours long.

This is a Jaguar XKR-S during a 2010 24 Hours of Le Mans race.

Formula One racecars look much different than cars used in Le Mans and GT races. This is a Jaguar Formula One racecar in a 2004 race.

The cars must go fast while racing but also be well made enough not to have any mechanical problems. Le Mans is a real test of a car's engineering and endurance. Car companies must have at least three drivers, who switch off driving during the race. That way no driver has to drive for too long.

From 2000 to 2004 Jaguar had a team in Formula One. Even though the team was named Jaguar and used Jaguar bodies, it used Ford engines because Ford owned Jaguar at the time.

XK120

The Jaguar XK120 was designed by William Lyons in 1948. He designed the car for a car show and meant to make only one. However, the car's sleek lines and powerful engine were such a hit that Lyons put it into production. The XK120 was given its name because it had a top speed of 120 miles per hour (193 km/h). That is fast now, but it was incredibly fast in 1948, when the car first came out. The XK120 was in production from 1948 until 1954.

This is a 1949 XK120 at an antique car show. It is a type of car called a roadster, which describes a roofless, open car.

1948 XK120

Engine size	3.4 liters
Number of cylinders	6
Transmission	Manual
Gearbox	4 speeds
0–62 mph (0–100 km/h)	9.9 seconds
Top speed	120 mph (193 km/h)

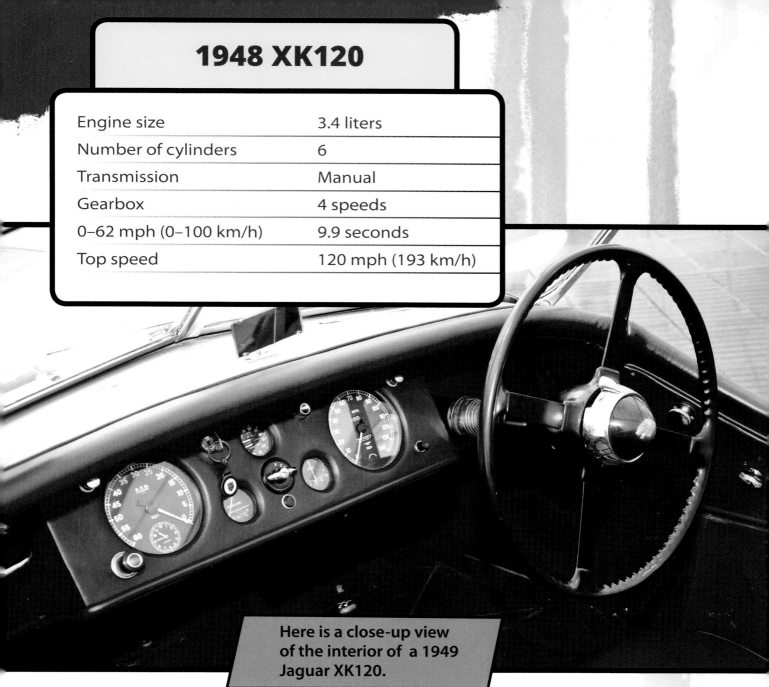

Here is a close-up view of the interior of a 1949 Jaguar XK120.

Its engine had 160 **horsepower**, which made it the most powerful engine in Europe at the time of its launch.

There was some worry that the production car could not live up to the speed of the original car. However, a Jaguar test driver demonstrated how fast the car could go. He actually got the car to go faster than 120 miles per hour (193 km/h). He reached a top speed of 136 miles per hour (219 km/h)!

E-Type

The Jaguar E-Type is a favorite of many car lovers. Even Enzo Ferrari, the owner of Jaguar's competitor, admired the E-Type. He was quoted as saying that it was "the most beautiful car ever made." The design of the E-Type was so highly thought of that it was put on display at the Museum of Modern Art, in New York City!

Unlike most models of the time, William Lyons did not design the E-Type. The man in charge of aerodynamics, Malcolm Sayer, designed it. The E-Type had a very long, slightly curved front. It was lower and slimmer than previous Jaguars. The design made the car very aerodynamic, which helped it go faster. It had a top speed of over 150 miles per hour (241 km/h). The E-Type was in production from 1961 until 1975.

The first series of Jaguar E-Type included the 1968 model, shown here.

1961 E-type

Engine size	3.8 liters
Number of cylinders	6
Transmission	Manual
Gearbox	4 speeds
0–62 mph (0–100 km/h)	7 seconds
Top speed	150 mph (241 km/h)

XJ

The Jaguar XJ began production in 1968 and continues to be made to this day. As the XJ was changed and updated over the years, it was released as a different series or as a model under the XJ name. The first XJ, the XJ6, was part of Series 1. The XJ6 was the last Jaguar designed by William Lyons. It was the car that he was most proud of. The XJ6 was a sedan. It had four doors and seats for passengers in the back. Most sports

This is a 2011 XJ.

XJ6

Engine size	1.2 liters
Number of cylinders	6
Transmission	Automatic
Gearbox	3 speeds
0–62 mph (0–100 km/h)	10.1 seconds
Top speed	120 mph (193 km/h)

The Jaguar XJ 220 shown here is a 1994 model.

cars have only two doors and space for the driver and one passenger. The XJ6 was powerful and fast, with a top speed of 120 miles per hour (193 km/h).

Over the years, the XJ evolved. Series 2 of the XJ began in 1973. Series 3 was produced from 1979 until 1992. The latest XJ model was launched in 2009 and is still in production. It is called the XJ351.

In 2011, Jaguar began racing in the American Le Mans. Jaguar had a history of success in the 24 Hours of Le Mans race, and in fact they were the most successful British car maker in that race's history. The car they raced with in the 2011 American Le Mans was the RSR XKR GT2. The Rocketsports Racing team worked with Jaguar to make this top-of-the-line racecar, which they drive in the race.

The RSR XKR GT2 was built in Michigan. It has a V8 engine, 550 horsepower, and a top speed of 180 miles per hour (128 km/h). The design of the body is based on the Jaguar XKR sports car. That means that the frame and skeleton of the car are the same as the XKR, but the engine is different. Special attention was paid to making this racing car very light and aerodynamic.

The Rocketsports Racing team drove this RSR XKR GT2 during their 2010 season.

RSR XKR GT2

Engine size	5 liters
Number of cylinders	8
Transmission	Manual
Gearbox	6 speeds
Top speed	180 mph (128 km/h)

XF

The Jaguar XF replaced an older Jaguar model, called the S-Type. It has the same interior and framework as the S-Type. The XF is a mid-size luxury sedan. It is made to give a smooth ride and be comfortable for passengers. It has four doors, seating for passengers in the back, and a large trunk. The XF is long, wide, and heavy. The XF was first shown in 2007 and went into production in 2008.

This is a 2011 Jaguar XF.

2013 XF

Engine size	2 liters
Number of cylinders	4
Transmission	Automatic
Gearbox	8 speeds
0–62 mph (0–100 km/h)	7.5 seconds
Top speed	121 mph (195 km/h)

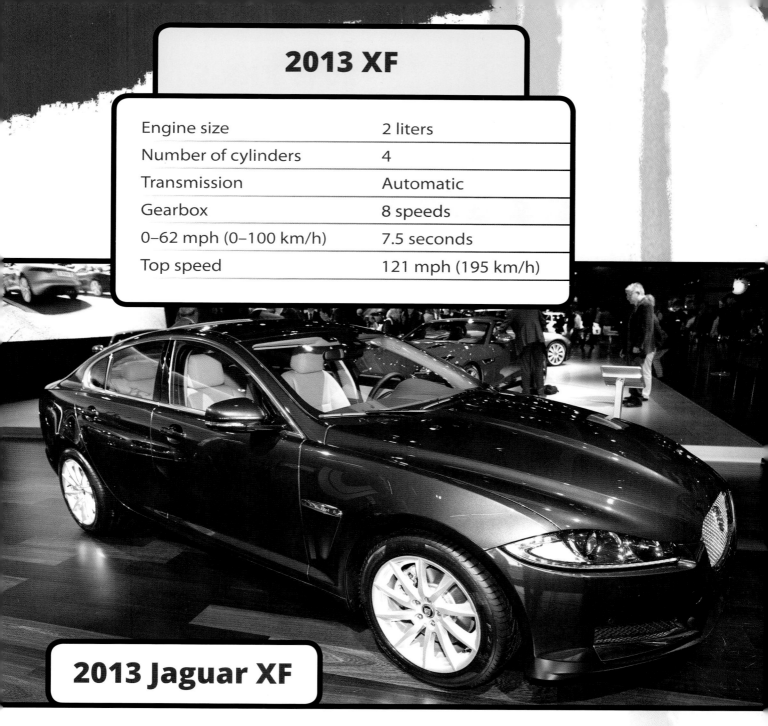

2013 Jaguar XF

The XF is still in production as of 2013. The XF comes with the option of a V6 or V8 engine. The 2013 XF has a top speed of 121 miles per hour (195 km/h) and can go from 0-62 miles per hour (0-100 km/h) in 7.5 seconds. Like all Jaguars, the 2013 Jaguar is sleek and aerodynamic. The interior of the XF is comfortable and stylish. Even though it is a larger, heavier car it is still fast and powerful.

2013 XKR-S

Engine size	5 liters
Number of cylinders	8
Transmission	Automatic
Gearbox	6 speeds
0–62 mph (0–100 km/h)	4.2 seconds
Top speed	186 mph (299 km/h)

The Jaguar XK is a series that was introduced in 1996. The first XK model, the XK8, was the first eight-cylinder car made by Jaguar. All XK models have two doors and long noses. XKs have the option of either being **coupes** or convertibles. A coupe is a car with a hard top. Convertibles have soft tops that can be rolled back.

This convertible version of the 2011 XK is being shown at a car show with its top down.

Top: This is the XK8 coupe. *Bottom*: Jaguar fans were happy that the XK's design, while new, still maintained the quiet elegance of a classic Jaguar design.

The XKR went into production in 2006 and is still being produced today. Ian Callum, who had become Jaguar's design director in 1999, designed the XKR. *Auto Express* magazine named the XKR "Car of the Year" in 2006. Auto Express also awarded Ian Callum "Person of the Year" in 2009 in part because of his work on the XKR.

The 2013 XKR-S is extremely fast and powerful. It has a V8 engine and a top speed of 186 miles per hour (299 km/h)! It is also available as a coupe or convertible.

Future of Jaguar

As Jaguar moves into the future, it must keep coming up with new, fast, and powerful cars. In 2013, Jaguar released the F-Type. The F-Type is a two-seat convertible. The F-Type comes in three different versions. They are the F-Type, the F-Type S, and the F-Type V8 S. The F-Type V8 S is the most powerful version. It has a top speed of 186 miles per hour (299 km/h). It can go from 0 to 60 miles per hour (0–96.5 km/h) in only 4.2 seconds.

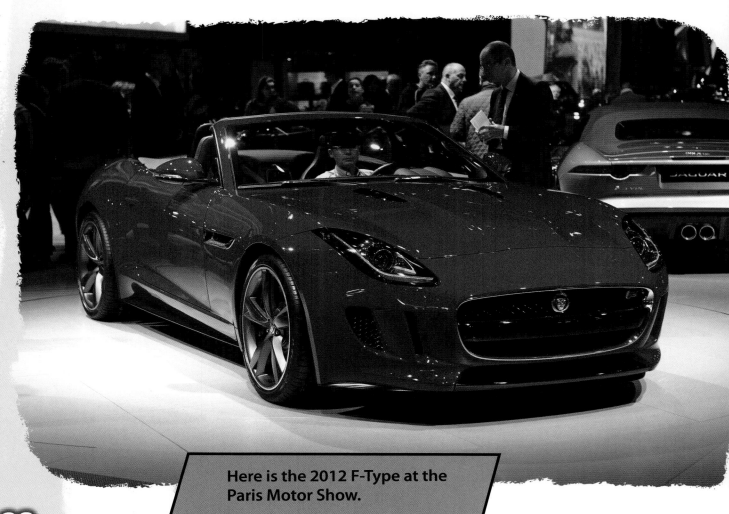

Here is the 2012 F-Type at the Paris Motor Show.

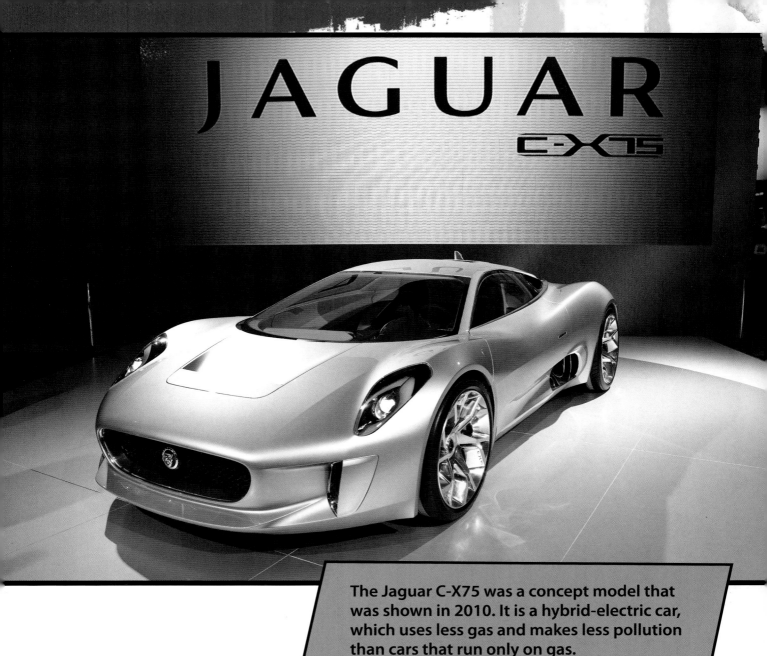

The Jaguar C-X75 was a concept model that was shown in 2010. It is a hybrid-electric car, which uses less gas and makes less pollution than cars that run only on gas.

Like all Jaguars, the F-Type will be stylish, fast, and elegant. Jaguar creates some of the most desirable cars in the world and has done so since 1931. The company has remained successful for so long by constantly innovating, yet remembering their roots in engineering and design.

Comparison Chart

CAR	YEARS MADE	SALES	TOP SPEED	FUN FACT
XK120	1948–1954	12,055	120 mph (193 km/h)	The racing version of the XK120, the XK120 C, won the 24 Hours of Le Mans in 1951 and 1953.
E-Type	1961–1975	72,500	150 mph (241 km/h)	This model was the fastest production car in the world in 1961.
XJ	1968–1992	402,848	120 mph (193 km/h)	The XJ made record-breaking sales for Jaguar.
RSR XKR GT2	2010–	n/a	180 mph (289 km/h)	This model was made in Michigan. Most Jaguars are made in Whitely, Coventry, England.
XF	2008–	n/a	121 mph (195 km/h)	The XF has no option for a cloth interior. All versions come with fully trimmed leather.
XK	1996–	n/a	186 mph (299 km/h)	The XK is made with an aluminum monocoque chassis.

Glossary

aerodynamic (er-oh-dy-NA-mik) Made to move through the air easily.

chassis (CHA-seez) Parts that hold up the body of a car.

coupes (KOOPS) Cars that have two doors and hard roofs.

cylinders (SIH-len-ders) The enclosed spaces for a piston in an engine.

design (dih-ZYN) The plan or the form of something.

endurance (en-DUR-ints) Strength and the ability to go long distances without getting tired easily.

evolved (ih-VOLVD) Changed over many years.

horsepower (HORS-pow-er) The way an engine's power is measured. One horsepower is the power to lift 550 pounds (250 kg) 1 foot (.3 m) in 1 second.

innovative (IH-nuh-vay-tiv) Having new things.

monocoque chassis (mon-uh-KOK CHA-see) A type of chassis that is of one piece with the body of the car.

production (pruh-DUK-shun) Made to sell.

sidecar (SYD-kar) A passenger seat that connects to a motorcycle.

technology (tek-NAH-luh-jee) Advanced tools that help people do and make things.

Index

Websites

Due to the changing nature of Internet links, PowerKids Press has developed an online list of websites related to the subject of this book. This site is updated regularly. Please use this link to access the list: www.powerkidslinks.com/smach/jag/